The Insider's Guide to the Air High School Studer.

2021-2022 Application Year Edition

Lieutenant Colonel Robert Kirkland, U.S. Army Retired

© 2021 Robert Kirkland

*If you would prefer a **PDF copy** of this book, you can purchase it at https://rotcconsulting.com under the Resources tab.*

Other Air Force ROTC Scholarship Resources available for purchase at https://rotcconsulting.com:

Air Force ROTC Scholarship Online Course: A step-by-step course to walk you through how to win an ROTC scholarship.

Full-Service Scholarship Preparation: work with the author and his team "start to finish" on your Air Force ROTC application (online course included in this service)

Interview Preparation

Essay Preparation

Premium Podcasts Episodes: On the interview and fitness test

College Incentive List: Full List of Air Force ROTC schools with room and board and in state tuition.

DODMERB Online Course: A step-by-step course on how to qualify medically for Air Force ROTC

Why did I decide to write this book?

Over the past four years, I have published a very well received guide for the Army ROTC High School Scholarship Program. When working with clients in obtaining the Army ROTC Scholarship, these same clients have asked for help in understanding other Service's high school scholarship programs.

Through my many connections in the Air Force, I decided to sit down and write a book that gave an "insiders" view of the Air Force High School Scholarship Program (HSSP). I talked extensively with current Professors of Aerospace Studies and other officers associated with the Air Force ROTC program to get the most accurate picture of how the selections process works. This book is a result of those conversations and research.

Like my book on Army ROTC scholarships, there is a lot of information about the Air Force HSSP in books, official Air Force websites, blogs and posting boards. However, there is not a source that I know of which gives you the specific, insider details on how the Air Force ROTC scholarship selection process works and what you can do to put yourself at the best advantage to win one of these valuable awards.

How this book is set up:

First, I assume that you understand the basics of Air Force ROTC. If you need an overview of the Air Force ROTC program, I would encourage you to visit their website at https://www.afrotc.com/

I have tried to include as much "official language" as possible in this book so that you understand, verbatim, the policies Air Force ROTC uses to select candidates for these scholarships.

After each modified "official" section or part, I provide you tips and commentary which are "insider tips." They are designated by the lightbulb icon:

I also provide helpful Appendices with documents which will further elaborate on my commentary or will prove helpful in better understanding how the scholarship program is administered.

It is my sincere hope that this book takes the mystery out of what it takes to win an Air Force ROTC scholarship. I wish you the best of luck in your quest to help pay for school with the goal of becoming an officer in the United States Air Force!

Lieutenant Colonel Robert Kirkland (U.S. Army, Retired) was the one of the few officers ever to command two separate Army ROTC programs—Claremont McKenna College from 2006 to 2009 and the University of Southern California from 2010 to 2013. He was selected as Army ROTC instructor of the year as well as the best Professor of Military Science in his Brigade in 2009. He is a graduate of the U.S. Military Academy, West Point and also has earned a MA and PhD from the University of Pittsburgh. He served over 25 years on active duty.

The author and his team at ROTC Consultants provide in depth, personal consulting and interview preparation to Air Force ROTC applicants. Visit their website at http://www.rotcconsulting.com for further information. They provide a full refund of all consulting fees if the applicant does not receive a scholarship. Please also see Appendix G for frequently asked questions about ROTC scholarship consulting.

Table of Contents

The Air Force ROTC Program and Scholarship

The purpose of the Air Force Reserve Officers Training Corps (AFROTC) is to provide an incentive to attract and retain high quality high school seniors and graduates whose leadership potential, personal and physical qualities, and academic specialties meet United States Air Force accession objectives.

Benefits

Indeed, the Air Force ROTC scholarships are one of the largest and most generous scholarship programs in the country. The scholarship types are tiered from a Type 1 that pays full tuition (no cap), to a Type 2 which has a $18,000 tuition cap, to a Type 7 which pays full tuition at the in-state tuition rate where the student qualifies for a receives in-state rate at a public school. In 2018, 69% of scholarships awarded are a Type 7, with 19% awarded at a Type 2 and the remaining 12% a Type 1. In the 2018 application year, 2,851 scholarships were offered out of 5,579 applications received.

Students receiving 4-Year Type 7 scholarships have the option of converting to a 3-Year Type 2 scholarship which begins in the candidate's sophomore year.

The following is a list of public universities that allow 4 Year Type 7 Out of State Residents the In-State tuition rate based on agreement between their Admissions Office and AF ROTC

University of Arkansas
Florida State University
University of Georgia
University of Iowa
Louisiana Tech University
Louisiana State University
University of Kansas
Kansas State University
University of Kentucky
Michigan Tech University
University of Minnesota
Mississippi State University
Missouri University of Science and Technology
University of Missouri
University of Nebraska-Lincoln
University of Nebraska-Omaha

North Dakota State University
University of North Dakota
Northern Illinois University
University of Oklahoma
Oklahoma State University
Rutgers University
University of Memphis
Angelo State University
University of Houston
Texas A&M University
Texas Tech University
University of North Texas
University of Texas-Austin
University of Texas San Antonio
West Virginia University

The average SAT/ACT score for winners in 2018 was: 1350 SAT, ACT 30, GPA 3.71.

All scholarship cadets also receive a living expense or subsistence allowance (stipend). The cadet earns different amounts depending on the level in the Air Force ROTC starting at $300 per month for the first year and peaking at $500 in the cadets'4th year.

Finally, a "flat rate" fee is paid for books, supplies and equipment. This is in addition to the tuition and fees or the room and board option. Currently, cadets receive $900 per year.

Many schools offer monetary offsets for room and board if a student is on an Air Force ROTC scholarship. Contact specific Air Force ROTC programs to see if their schools offer monetary or other type incentives to scholarship cadets. The author also has a list by each Air Force ROTC program. For a small fee, you can buy the list on his website: https://rotcconsulting.com/resources/college-incentives-rotc-programs/

The Air Force ROTC scholarship program has been "missioned" to ensure that scholarships are awarded to specific academic disciplines.

The most highly desired majors for AFROTC cadets are listed below. These majors receive 80% of the scholarship allocation:

Aeronautical Engineering
Aerospace Engineering
Architectural Engineering
Architecture
Astronautical Engineering
Chemistry
Civil Engineering
Computer Engineering
Computer Science
Electrical Engineering
Environmental Engineering
Mathematics
Mechanical Engineering
Meteorological/Atmospheric Science
Nuclear Engineering
Nuclear Physics
Operations Research
Physics

In recent years, the Air Force has placed great value in language skills and now awards about 10% of the remaining scholarship allocation to the following strategic language majors:

Arabic
Baluchi
Chinese, Amoy
Chinese, Cantonese
Chinese, Mandarin
Chinese, Wu
Indonesian
Japanese
Javanese
Korean
Pashto-Afghan
Persian-Afghan
Persian-Iranian
Punjabi
Russian
Somali
Swahili
Turkish
Turkmen

In order to receive a scholarship, you need to strongly consider majoring in one of the above technical fields first. Strategic languages is a second option. Very few scholarships (10%) are awarded outside of these fields (including nursing).

General Eligibility

To be eligible for the Air Force ROTC Four-Year College Scholarship, you must meet the following general eligibility requirements:

- You must be a U.S. citizen.

- At least 17 years of age prior to scholarship activation.

- Under 31 years of age by December 31st of the year in which they will commission. If the applicant has prior active-duty service, this limit may be extended.

- Be a high school graduate.

- Have a minimum high school Cumulative Unweighted Grade Point Average (GPA) of 3.0 at the completion of the 11th grade.

- Receive a minimum SAT score of 1240 or an ACT composite score of 26.

- You must have no moral obligation or personal conviction that will prevent you from supporting and defending the Constitution of the United States against all enemies and conscientiously bearing arms.

- Satisfactorily explain any record of arrest and/or civil conviction.

Obligations

If you are awarded a scholarship, you become obligated when you accept and sign an agreement with the United States Air Force. If you are under legal age in the state where the school is located, your parent or legal guardian signs this agreement.
You will agree to:

- Enroll in the academic major for which the scholarship is offered.
- Enroll in Air Force ROTC beginning in the fall term.

- Complete a 24-day summer field training course at Maxwell Air Force Base, Alabama (usually between your sophomore and junior years).
- Complete Air Force ROTC General Military Course (GMC) your freshman and sophomore years and the Professional Officer Course (POC) your junior and senior years.
- Accept a commission as an Air Force Officer and serve at least four years on active duty.

Keep in mind that a cadet is evaluated at the end of their sophomore year to determine if he/she will continue in the Air Force ROTC program. This evaluation is based on performance as a cadet. If a student is not selected to continue in the program, their scholarship will be terminated. In 2018, about 10% of cadets did not progress to their third year. This varies from year to year.

For can find a copy of the contract you will sign upon accepting the scholarship in Appendix A. You can also obtain the contract (AF1056) at http://www.e-publishing.af.mil/

ROTC Program Personnel

Before we continue with the discussion of how you are selected for a scholarship, it is important to know who you will be interacting with at a college or university Air Force ROTC program while going through the application process. The following are key people you should become familiar with:

- Professor of Aerospace Studies: This is an Air Force Officer, normally a lieutenant colonel or colonel, who is the senior representative at the college or university for the ROTC program. He supervises the recruiting, training and commissioning of officer candidates.

- Recruiting Flight Commander: This is an Air Force Officer, normally a captain or major who runs the day to day recruitment of students into the program to include executing the scholarship program. He is your first point of contact when you have specific questions about the ROTC before you arrive as a student on campus. Supervised by the Professor of Aerospace Studies.

- Non-Commissioned Officer in Charge: Normally a technical sergeant, he is the senior non-commissioned officer in the program. Reports directly to the Professor of Aerospace Studies on all matters of training.

Selection Criteria

Air Force ROTC states that all factors are important and are considered in the selection of scholarship winners.   However, some factors are more important than others.

Air Force ROTC ranks scholarship applicants based on a thousand-point scale:

Area of Consideration	Points
Interview	450
Unweighted GPA	200
SATe (SAT/ACT)	300
Physical Fitness Assessment	50
Total Points	*1000*

The AFROTC Interview---450 Points

Air Force ROTC considers the personal interview to be the most critical aspect of selection process and the weight of the point totals back this up. The Interview is used to assess officership and leadership potential by discerning alignment of student's values with Air Force character/core values, self-confidence, human relations predisposition, planning and organizing ability, communication skills, leadership ability, motivation toward the Air Force, demonstrated ability to get things done and to be successful, assessment of the applicants ability to control situations with their presence and speaking ability, assessment of how well the applicant will fit into the Air Force and military lifestyle and level of physical fitness.

Achievement in extracurricular activities (vice mere participation) is a key indicator of leadership and officer potential. Extracurricular activities include athletics, academic, civic organizations, student government, employment, etc.

If you are selected as a scholarship finalist, you will be directed through a notification letter. This will most likely be your geographically closest ROTC detachment to your home address. Any travel to and from the interview will be at your own expense.

Some of the things you can do to improve your interview score are the following:

- <u>STUDY</u> the types of questions and the criteria Air Force ROTC will use to score your interview that are found in this book.

- Bring a copy of your resume and list of leadership and activities.

- Understand the Air Force ROTC program and the U.S. Air Force. Do your research before you arrive. Websites such as https://www.afrotc.com/ https://www.afrotc.com/careers and http://www.af.mil go into depth about ROTC and the Air Force. Talk to current or former Air Force officers. Visit a local Air Force base or Air National Guard/Air Force Reserve base if you can. Mention you have done so in your interview. Get interview coaching from the author and his team (http://www.rotcconsulting.com)

- If possible, visit the ROTC program closed to your home of record before the interview. This shows that you are interested in ROTC and have spoken to cadets and instructors.

- Dress to impress. Ask the point of contact on the interview letter for preferences in this regard. In most cases, it is better to be overdressed than underdressed.

Day of the Interview

The interviewer will first give an overview of the ROTC program to the candidate.

Interviewers are instructed to emphasize to the applicant that any drug use (including marijuana) <u>after</u> the date of the interview is considered post-orientation and will render him/her ineligible for the Air Force.

Detachments will not conduct any type of Physical Fitness Assessment as part of the interview and subsequent evaluation. Detachments will perform a height and weight check during the interview but cannot conduct a body fat measurement for any applicants.

The Interview is scored in seven (7) topical areas as well as an overall recommendation score with the following point total breakout:

Interview Area	Points
Overall Recommendation for Selection	150
A-Character/Core Values	60
B-Self-Confidence	30
C-Human Relations	30

D-Planning and Organizing	40
E-Communicative Skills	60
F-Leadership	60
G-Motivation Toward Air Force	20
Total Points	*450*

Along with a score, the interviewer will also write one to two bullet comments per topical area. A list of possible interview questions for each area is located in Appendix C.

Overall Recommendation for Selection. The overall recommendation rating is based on the sum of the applicant's responses to the questions posed, the manner in which the applicant conducted themselves during the interview, the interviewer's experience as AFROTC Cadre or Admissions Liaison Officer, and his/her experience as an Air Force officer. Basically, it asks how strongly the interviewer recommends the applicant a scholarship?

Rating (Choose only one)	Benchmarks for: **Overall Recommendation- 150 Points**
Score=30	Applicant assessed as incompatible w/meeting minimum AFROTC standards. Not recommended for scholarship.
Score=60	Highly doubt applicant will make it through the first year of AFROTC. Below average candidate; significant weakness should preclude offer.
Score=90	Applicant might be able to complete AFROTC, but will need significant work. Average candidate; meets standards. Some leadership experience; Some weaknesses evident; Offer if Meets Needs of AF or Consider for Scholarship.
Score=120	Applicant would be great fit; visualize them successfully completing AFROTC. Above-average candidate; very competitive. Outstanding in some dimensions. Offer Scholarship.
Score=150	Would love to have this applicant at a detachment; competitive for top tier. An exceptional candidate; outstanding in most or all dimensions. Definitely Offer Scholarship.

A. Character/Core Values: Military officers do the right thing for the right reasons, all the time. It means doing the right thing whether someone is watching or not. They are loyal first to the Constitution and nation, then to the institutional Air Force, then to their units, then to their wingmen, and finally to themselves. They do not tolerate deviations from what is right from subordinates, peers, superiors or friends.

The main question the interviewer is attempting to answer here is how well the applicant will <u>fit into AFROTC and the Air Force</u>. Can the interviewer envision the applicant in an Air Force uniform, embracing Air Force values, willing to cede the individual liberty required of a military professional?

Rating (Choose only one)	Benchmarks for: **Character/Core Values- 60 Points**
Score=12	**Unsatisfactory**. Demonstrated poor character—lacks an understanding of integrity or lives in a way inconsistent with it; would be judged as rejecting AF core values
Score=24	**Marginal**. Demonstrated barely adequate character—has a shallow understanding of integrity and occasionally lives according to that understanding; would be judged as occasionally accepting of AF core values
Score=36	**Satisfactory**. Demonstrated adequate character—has an acceptable understanding of integrity and mostly lives according to that understanding; would be judged as mostly accepting of AF core values
Score=48	**Exceptional**. Demonstrates good character—has a sound understanding of integrity and lives according to that understanding; would be judged as generally accepting AF core values
Score=60	**Outstanding**. Demonstrates excellent character—has an advanced understanding of integrity and lives according to that understanding; would be judged as virtually always accepting of AF core values

B. Self Confidence: Military officers are self-confident. They are confident in their ability to accomplish assigned missions and their ability to control themselves. They project a calm, unflappable, martial image regardless how challenging the environment so as to inspire confidence among their subordinates. Military officers know how to be, and are, in charge when appropriate.

The main question the interviewer is attempting to answer is how the applicant holds him or herself, maintains eye contact, interacts with, and speaks to the interviewer. The candidate should demonstrate confidence and advanced social skills. They should be comfortable with the interviewer, be judged assertive and competitive, and seem to be high- energy optimists. The interviewer should not have to pull out answers from the candidate.

Rating (Choose only one)	Benchmarks for: **Self Confidence- 30 points**
Score=6	**Unsatisfactory**. Demonstrated poor self-confidence—slouched; nervous and ill-at-ease; avoided eye contact; quavering voice, volunteered little information; timid during introduction, did not offer handshake or identify themselves
Score=12	**Marginal**. Demonstrated barely adequate self-confidence—tended to slouch, almost blended into the background; occasionally maintained eye contact, frequently averted their gaze; voice was low when responding, had to ask them to speak up; volunteered some information; hesitated during introduction, shook hands
Score=18	**Satisfactory**. Demonstrated adequate self-confidence—average bearing/posture, occasionally slouched; worked at maintaining eye contact; verbal delivery was generally good, halting at times; volunteered some information; generally overcame anxiety during introduction
Score=24	**Exceptional**. Demonstrated good self-confidence—above average bearing/posture; generally maintained eye contact; very good verbal delivery, occasionally spoke fast; able to discuss personal accomplishments; assertive at times; good introduction
Score=30	**Outstanding**. Demonstrated excellent self-confidence—stood and sat tall, leaned forward to engage with interviewer; maintained constant eye contact; clear and well-paced verbal delivery; provided complete answers with examples to questions; very assertive, but appropriate; firm handshake and forceful introduction

C. Human Relations: Military officers are comfortable working in teams and they value the inherent strengths that come from teams made up of people with different backgrounds and perspectives. They are respectful of others. They understand that high performing teams are characterized by common goals, shared responsibility for success and appropriate leadership-followership relationships.

The main question the interviewer is attempting to answer is how skilled a leader the candidate is. The candidate should be able to cite several examples of instances where he/she has influenced and/or directed others to accomplish a task. The candidate will be able to describe task that needed to be done, how he/she worked through others to take the action needed to get it done, and the impact of accomplishing the task. The focus is on *influencing others to get something done.*

Rating (Choose only one)	Benchmarks for: **Human Relations- 30 Points**
Score=6	**Unsatisfactory**. Demonstrated inadequate human relations skills—a loner, poor team-player; intolerant of other people and their views; values personal success over group success and mission accomplishment, it's all about them.
Score=12	**Marginal**. Demonstrated barely adequate human relations skills—prefers working alone, even when a group might produce a better outcome; has some difficulty respecting other viewpoints; believes that by taking care of themselves they will be taking care of the group.
Score=18	**Satisfactory**. Demonstrated adequate human relations skills—prefers working alone, but is comfortable in group setting; tolerant of others and their views; helpful in achieving group goals; accepts the notion that individual differences improve group performance but cannot cite an example where they have experienced it.
Score=24	**Exceptional**. Demonstrated good human relations skills—prefers working with others rather than of alone when the task permits; relates well with and respects others; generally concerned with advancing group goals as a way of advancing their personal goals; has experienced the benefit of differing perspectives during group problem-solving.
Score=30	**Outstanding**. Demonstrated excellent human relations skills—consummate team-player, significant experience working with others and advancing group goals; genuinely concerned with and respectful of others and these perspectives are apparent in how they related to the interviewer; embraces the differences in people and values the inherent strength of complementary perspectives found in a work group.

D. Planning and Organizing: Military officers get things done. They are able determine how best to divide large tasks into smaller parts and then develop plans to accomplish them. They are able to set priorities and manage their time accordingly, then organize themselves and others to accomplish the priority tasks. Then, they relentlessly apply themselves until they get the job done.

The main question the interviewer is attempting to answer is how driven the candidate is to accomplish assigned tasks or goals to the best of his/her ability. These candidates are often described as responsible, dependable, or ethical professionals who have an exceptional work ethic. They are good planners, for whom initiative is a strong suit; they have an intrinsic need to achieve. The focus of these bullets is on *doing what it takes to get something done.*

Rating (Choose only one)	Benchmarks for: **Planning and Organizing- 40 points**
Score=8	**Unsatisfactory**. Demonstrated poor planning and organizing skills—could not identify a single instance when they had successfully planned, organized and accomplished a significant project. Unable to prioritize tasks and manage time.
Score=16	**Marginal**. Demonstrated barely adequate planning and organizing skills—gave one example of having planned and organized to accomplish a task. Unconvincing regarding ability to prioritize tasks, manage time and demonstrate a willingness to work hard to get a project done.
Score=24	**Satisfactory**. Demonstrated adequate planning and organizing skills—a few examples of having developed plans to accomplish tasks, organized to do so, then set priorities and managed their time to accomplish these tasks. Generally worked on the projects until completion.
Score=32	**Exceptional**. Demonstrated good planning and organizing skills—several examples of having developed solid plans to accomplish significant tasks, organized well, then generally set useful priorities to accomplish these tasks and managed their time accordingly. Persistently worked on the projects until completion.
Score=40	**Outstanding**. Demonstrated excellent planning and organizing skills—many examples of having developed excellent plans to accomplish significant tasks; of having organized appropriately; then set insightful priorities to accomplish these tasks, while they ruthlessly managed their time accordingly. Relentlessly worked on the projects until completion.

E. Communication Skills: Military officers are clear verbal communicators. They recognize that clear communication requires effective listening, careful thought, and articulate and appropriate responses. They have an exceptional verbal delivery.

The main question the interviewer is attempting to answer is how skilled a leader the candidate is. The candidate should be able to cite several examples of instances where he/she has influenced and/or directed others to accomplish a task. The candidate will be able to describe task that needed to be done, how he/she worked through others to take the action needed to get it done, and the impact of accomplishing the task. The focus is on *influencing others to get something done.*

Rating (Choose only one)	Benchmarks for: **Communication Skills- 60 Points**
Score=12	**Unsatisfactory**. Demonstrated poor communication skills—failed to listen to questions or didn't understand them and gave an inappropriate responses; spoke without thinking, rambled on without a point; inarticulate, poor vocabulary/mostly slang; very poor verbal delivery—tone of voice, pace of delivery, annunciation
Score=24	**Marginal**. Demonstrated barely adequate communication skills—seemed to listen to questions and understand them but gave inappropriate responses; frequently spoke without thinking; relatively inarticulate—groped for the correct word, below average vocabulary/frequently used slang; poor verbal delivery—tone of voice, pace of delivery, annunciation
Score=36	**Satisfactory**. Demonstrated adequate communication skills—seemed to listen to the questions; sometimes thought before speaking, other times not; some of the time gave well-conceived and appropriate response, other times not; somewhat articulate, occasional use of slang; acceptable verbal delivery—tone of voice, pace of delivery, annunciation
Score=48	**Exceptional**. Demonstrated good communication skills—listened to the questions; generally thought before speaking; generally gave well-conceived and appropriate response; articulate, rare use of slang; good verbal delivery—tone of voice, pace of delivery, annunciation
Score=60	**Outstanding**. Demonstrated excellent communication skills—listened intently to the questions; gathered their thoughts; gave well-conceived and appropriate responses; very articulate, similar to speaking with a college professor; exceptional verbal delivery—tone of voice, pace of delivery, annunciation

F. Leadership: Military officers are effective leaders. They are skilled at influencing and directing others in order to accomplish a task. They have a knack for employing group problem-solving, developing commitment from teammates, delegating and following-up on tasks, and motivating the people they work with to accomplish a group goal.

The main question the interviewer is attempting to answer is how skilled a leader the candidate is. The candidate should be able to cite several examples of instances where he/she has influenced and/or directed others to accomplish a task. The candidate will be able to describe task that needed to be done, how he/she worked through others to take the action needed to get it done, and the impact of accomplishing the task. The focus is on *influencing others to get something done.*

Rating (Choose only one)	Benchmarks for: **Leadership- 60 Points**
Score=12	**Unsatisfactory**. Demonstrated poor leadership skills— Does not have any leadership experience; shows no initiative; does not accept responsibility; reluctant to make decisions; no attempts to influence/direct others to accomplish a task.
Score=24	**Marginal**. Demonstrated barely adequate leadership skills — Limited leadership experience; shows little initiative; reluctantly accepts responsibility; few attempts to influence/direct others to accomplish a task.
Score=36	**Satisfactory**. Demonstrated adequate leadership skills — Some leadership experience; displays some initiative; accepts responsibility, but generally does not seek out leadership roles; sometimes influences/directs others to accomplish a task.
Score=48	**Exceptional**. Demonstrated good leadership skills — Significant leadership experience; high degree of initiative; seeks out leadership roles by volunteering and accepts responsibility; frequently influences/directs others to accomplish a task.
Score=60	**Outstanding**. Demonstrated excellent leadership skills — Outstanding leadership experience; initiative personified; eagerly seeks out responsibility/leadership roles; consistently influences/directs others to accomplish a task.

G. Motivation toward the Air Force: The path to an Air Force officer's commission through AFROTC is challenging. A cadet has to complete a rigorous undergraduate program while they are learning the distinctly military elements of their chosen career. Success takes drive and motivation.

The main question the interviewer is attempting to answer here is how well the applicant will fit into AFROTC and the Air Force. Can the interviewer envision the applicant in an Air Force uniform, embracing Air Force values, willing to cede the individual liberty required of a military professional?

Also, the interviewer will get a sense of the fitness-level and professional appearance of the applicant. This can be surmised through applicant disclosure of the physical fitness test score, participation in sports and personal appearance.

If the applicant is overweight (based on the height/weight table below), the interviewer must indicate if they are in-shape (i.e.: muscular athlete) or out of shape (i.e.: judging by appearance, does not meet body fat standard). Importantly, if the applicant had a waiver for the Physical Fitness Assessment, the interviewer must indicate what prevented the applicant from taking the assessment (fitness test waived due to sprained ankle, but highly fit track star) and the interviewer must also indicate if he/she thinks they will meet weight standards. If the applicant scored poorly on the fitness test, the interviewer must address it and indicate what the applicant is doing to improve in that area.

Height (inches)	Minimum Weight (lbs)	Maximum Weight (lbs)
58	91	119
59	94	124
60	97	128
61	100	132
62	104	136
63	107	141
64	110	145
65	114	150
66	117	155
67	121	159
68	125	164
69	128	169
70	132	174
71	136	179
72	140	184
73	144	189
74	148	194
75	152	200
76	156	205
77	160	210
78	164	216
79	168	221
80	173	227

Rating (Choose only one)	Benchmarks for: Motivation toward the Air Force- 20 Points
Score=4	**Unsatisfactory.** Low-level of motivation toward the USAF; uninterested; no real desire to be interviewed.
Score=8	**Marginal.** Lukewarm; non-committal; very little thought on what

	he/she wants to accomplish in AFROTC or USAF.
Score=12	**Satisfactory.** Interested in the Air Force, but mostly interested in scholarship; willing to accept ADSC in return for scholarship; good understanding of the requirements of AFROTC program and military service.
Score=16	**Exceptional.** Very interested in military service; wants to make good impression; knows the requirements of AFROTC program and military service.
Score=20	**Outstanding.** Enthusiastic and highly motivated about becoming Air Force officer; came prepared to impress and did; fully aware of the requirements of AFROTC program and military service.

Again, the interview is <u>by far</u> the most important part of the application. Understand the areas that ROTC is concerned about and read over the questions they will ask you in Appendix C. Be prepared! Get interview coaching from ROTC consultants.

Grade Point Average. 200 Points.

Point total is unweighted GPA multiplied by 50. The GPA is calculated from the applicant's freshman to junior year.

Unweighted GPA	Points
4.0	200
3.9	195
3.8	190
3.7	185
3.6	180
3.5	175
3.4	170
3.3	165
3.2	160
3.1	155
3.0	150
2.9	145
2.8	140
2.7	135
2.6	130
2.5	125

2.4	120
2.3	115
2.2	110

 The average unweighted high school GPA of scholarship winners was 3.8

College Board Scores.   300 Points.

When more than one set of SAT/ACT scores are available, the highest scores from <u>one sitting</u> will be used.

The following is how a maximum of 300 points would be calculated:
College Board Scores

SAT Score	Points	ACT Score
1240	232	26
1250	234	
1260	236	
1270	238	
1280	240	27
1290	242	
1300	244	
1310	245	
1320	247	28
1330	249	
1340	251	
1350	253	29
1360	255	
1370	257	
1380	259	
1390	260	30
1400	262	
1410	264	
1420	266	31
1430	268	
1440	270	
1450	272	32
1460	274	
1470	275	
1480	277	
1490	279	33

1500	281	
1510	283	
1520	285	34
1530	287	
1540	289	
1550	290	
1560	292	35
1570	294	
1580	296	
1590	298	
1600	300	36

There is no penalty for taking the SAT or ACT as many times as you want. The highest scores are taken from the "best sitting" so there nothing to lose by doing poorly on a subsequent test.

Before you spend the money on retaking these tests, determine realistically how many points you would gain by retaking either test. If you don't think you will raise your score significantly, then save your money.

Physical Fitness Assessment-- 50 Points

The Air Force Fitness Test, known as the Physical Fitness Assessment (PFA) is the same as given to members of the Air Force. It is conducted by a high school official such as your gym coach and must be completed by January 2021.

The following is the test and scoring:

The AFROTC Scholarship Physical Fitness Assessment is a 1 minute timed event for both pushups and sit-ups and a 1.5-mile run. The instructional scorecard is found on the electronic application.

Here is the point scale for the test.

Score	Points
Greater than 70	50
68-70	45

66-67.9	40
64-65.9	35
62-63.9	30
60-61.9	25
58-59.9	20
56-57.9	15
54-55.9	10
52-53.9	5
51.9 or Less	0

Male					
Push Ups		Sit Ups		1.5 Mile Run	
Reps	Score	Reps	Score	Time	Score
>67	10	>58	10	<9:12	60
62	9.5	55	9.5	9:13-9:34	59.7
61	9.4	54	9.4	9:35-9:45	59.3
60	9.3	53	9.2	9:46-9:58	58.9
59	9.2	52	9.0	9:59-10:10	58.5
58	9.1	51	8.8	10:11-10:23	57.9
57	9.0	50	8.7	10:24-10:37	57.3
56	8.9	49	8.5	10:38-10:51	56.6
55	8.8	48	8.3	10:52-11:06	55.7
54	8.8	47	8.0	11:07-11:22	54.8
53	8.7	46	7.5	11:23-11:38	53.7
52	8.6	45	7.0	11:39-11:56	52.4
51	8.5	44	6.5	11:57-12:14	50.9
50	8.4	43	6.3	12:15-12:33	49.2
49	8.3	42	6.0	12:34-12:53	47.2
48	8.1	>42	0	12:54-13:14	44.9
47	8.0			13:15-13:36	42.3
46	7.8			13:37-	0
45	7.7				
44	7.5				
43	7.3				
42	7.2				
41	7.0				
40	6.8				
39	6.5				
38	6.3				
37	6.0				
36	5.8				
35	5.5				
34	5.3				

33	5.0				
>33	**0**				

		Female			
Push Ups		Sit Ups		1.5 Mile Run	
Reps	Score	Reps	Score	Time	Score
>47	10	>54	10	<10:23	60
42	9.5	51	9.5	10:24-10:51	49
41	9.4	50	9.4	10:52-11:06	48
40	9.3	49	9.0	11:07-11:22	47
39	9.2	48	8.9	11:23-11:38	46
38	9.1	47	8.8	11:39-11:56	45
37	9.0	46	8.6	11:57-12:14	44
36	8.9	45	8.5	12:15-12:33	43
35	8.8	44	8.0	12:34-12:53	42
34	8.6	43	7.8	12:54-13:14	41
33	8.5	42	7.5	13:15-13:36	40
32	8.4	41	7.0	13:37-14:00	39
31	8.3	40	6.8	14:01-14:25	38
30	8.2	39	6.5	14:26-14:52	37
29	8.1	38	6.0	14:53-15:20	36
28	8.0	>38	**0**	15:21-15:50	35
27	7.5			15:51-16:22	34
26	7.3			**16:23-**	**0**
25	7.2				
24	7.0				
23	6.5				
22	6.3				
21	6.0				
20	5.8				
19	5.5				
18	5.0				
>18	**0**				

Clearly, a candidate should concentrate on improving their run time over push-ups or sit ups as it counts for six times more in the composite score than either pushups or sit-ups. There is a large composite score increase if you can "max out" the run.

There are many sites that provide good advice on how to prepare for the fitness test. The best way to prepare for the test is to practice the actual exercises under timed conditions.

Another great resource is the services of Stew Smith. He is a former Navy Lieutenant (SEAL) who graduated from the United States Naval Academy and Basic Underwater Demolition/SEAL (BUD/S) training. He has been personally training, testing, and writing workout books and ebooks that prepare people to ace fitness tests for over 25 years. Consult his website at http://www.stewsmithfitness.com for more information

Online Application Steps

Now that you know how ROTC determines your overall score, it is important to understand how to fill out the online application.

Here are the steps:

Step 1: Create an Air Force Account at https://www.afrotc.com/scholarships

Step 2: Log into your Air Force ROTC Account. Complete and Submit the "My Profile" page

Step 3: Complete the My AFROTC Application Checklist, to include the activity sheet.

Step 4: Download and print the Counselor Certification Form. Scan and upload the signed counselor certification form and a copy of your official or unofficial high school transcript (must include the 9th-11th grade) the application

Step 5: Download and print a copy of the Physical Fitness Assessment (PFA) worksheet. Take a copy of the PFA worksheet with you when you complete the fitness assessment. Have the examiner fill in all of the information on the form and have him/her sign and date it. After you have completed the fitness assessment, use the worksheet to enter your results electronically. Scan and upload the completed worksheet to the application.

Step 6: Enter your GPA manually in the fields provided on the application and submit SAT and/or ACT scores electronically through the testing agency using AFROTC Test Code 0548. Enter your GPA electronically in the fields provided.

Step 7: The entire application must be complete by January 14, 2021. After you have completed the application steps and have met all qualifications, a local Air Force ROTC detachment will contact you to schedule an interview with an Air Force officer. Your application will be reviewed by the next available selection board to determine whether or not you will be offered a scholarship.

Application Deadlines

Must be submitted electronically by January 13, 2022. All additional documents such as transcripts, SAT/ACT scores, activity sheet, and fitness test scores must be uploaded. Applications will be rolled over to the next board is the applicant is not selected on an earlier board.

There are a number of components to a complete application. Remember that it is your responsibility, not your high school counselor or fitness test grader, to ensure that your application is complete.

Selection Boards

Air Force ROTC conducts three selection boards. The board dates are scheduled for 18-22 October 2021, 21-25 February 2022, and 21-25 March 2022. The March board will only convene if needed.

The application cut off deadline for each board is: 15 October, 18 February, and 18 March.

Board results are released within 14 days after the board concludes. A candidate must meet all scholarship eligibility criteria to include a scholarship interview with the nearest Air Force ROTC unit in order to be considered by the board. https://www.afrotc.com/scholarships/eligibility

Application Status

Air Force ROTC will contact you periodically about your status, and you can track your application status online. After you submit your application, you will be notified via email of your eligibility status. If you have not heard anything within six weeks, contact AFROTC at 866-423-7682 or email your scholarship technician.

It is critical that your current mailing address, email address and telephone number are accurate and updated on your application.

Notification of Winners:

You will notified by letter that you have won an Air Force ROTC scholarship between November 2021 and April 2022. The letter will indicate if you received a Type 1, 2 or 7 and if it is a technical, language, or non-technical major.

If you receive a Type 7 you will also be given the option to convert the scholarship to a 3 year Type 2.

💡 It is incumbent on the candidate to gain college admittance in the designated major on the notification letter and meet all deadlines.

💡 Service Academy Forums has some helpful tips on how to best financially leverage Type 2 and 7 scholarships. Your first stop, however, should be at the financial aid office of your colleges of interest.
http://www.serviceacademyforums.com/index.php?threads/just-recieved-official-afrotc-scholarship-letter-and-need-help.18384/

Other considerations:

Once you get on campus:

All scholarship applicants must successfully complete the Air Force Fitness Test at the minimum level in order to receive scholarship benefits (known as "contracting"). If the 4 year scholarship applicant does not pass fitness test by a pre-determined date (usually late December) of their freshman year, the scholarship offer will be withdrawn.

💡 Make sure you are in good physical condition when you come onto campus and can pass fitness test on the first try!

Medical Exams

Medical condition is not a consideration in the selection of scholarship winners; however, all winners must be medically qualified in order to contract as scholarship cadets and receive benefits. Scholarship recipients will be contacted via email to schedule a medical exam within two weeks of the offer email.

Individuals selected as scholarship finalists will be contacted and scheduled for a medical examination by the Department of Defense Medical Examination Review Board (DoDMERB). DoDMERB will normally contact students via letter or postcard announcing an appointment date and time or requesting that you contact a contracted physician to make an appointment. This process will be started upon acceptance the scholarship.

If the 4 year scholarship applicant is not medically qualified by late December of their freshman year, the scholarship offer <u>will be withdrawn</u>.

Appendix E shows the medical qualification flow chart.

You <u>can</u> receive a waiver from Air Force ROTC if you are disqualified by DODMERB for a medical condition. Again, refer to the Appendix E flow chart. Once you receive an Air Force ROTC waiver for the disqualifying condition, you are considered medically qualified.

The main conditions for which candidates receive a DODMERB disqualification are for: asthma (after 13th birthday), mental health, vision, hearing, orthodontics, and orthopedics. DODMERB medical examiners use the Department of Defense Instruction 6130.03 to determine if a candidate is medically disqualified for a condition. You can find this instruction at: http://www.med.navy.mil/sites/nmotc/nami/arwg/Documents/WaiverGuide/DODI_6130.03_JUL12.pdf

Air Force ROTC grants the most medical waivers for the following conditions: history of asthma, history of mental health problems, PRK/Lasik, orthodontics, and orthopedics. Medical waivers by ROTC are generally approved if the medical condition is static and will not be aggravated by military training and duties after commissioning. The condition <u>must not</u> prevent the person to deploy to a combat environment. The approval rate for waivers is based on the seriousness of the condition and needs of the Air Force.

You must comply as quickly as possible with any requirements to provide additional medical documents or to schedule a consultation in a particular area in order to avoid delays in a medical determination.

The DODMERB website has a great deal of information on the medical review process. https://dodmerb.tricare.osd.mil/Default.aspx. The Recruiting Flight Officer at your ROTC detachment of choice can also answer any questions you may have. Be sure to keep him updated on your medical qualification status!

Your <u>goal</u> is to be medically qualified before you come to campus in the fall. Do not wait until you arrive at campus to work through any medical issues. Again, keep your ROTC program of choice updated regarding your medical qualification.

Final Words

As you can tell, there are a lot of details and considerations that go into applying for and winning an Air Force ROTC scholarship. It is crucial that you become educated about the process and set yourself up the best you can in order to win one of these valuable awards.

If you follow the advice in this book, it _will_ significantly increase your chances of winning a scholarship. Following even one piece of advice could be the difference between a 4-year scholarship award and not getting an offer.

Keep in contact with your ROTC programs of interest during this process. The Recruiting Flight Commander at your detachment of choice will be glad to answer any question you may have.

I wish you the best of luck in your pursuit of these scholarships and your honorable goal of becoming officers in the U.S. Air Force!

The author provides in depth, personal consulting to ROTC applicants and their parents. Website: http://www.rotcconsulting.com. Please also see Appendix G for frequently asked questions about ROTC scholarship consulting.

Appendix A Air Force ROTC Scholarship Contract

AIR FORCE RESERVE OFFICER TRAINING CORPS *(AFROTC)* CONTRACT

PRIVACY ACT STATEMENT

AUTHORITY: 5 USC §14c, 10 USC Sections 2005 and 2103-2110; 50 App USC 456; and EO 9397. This is Executive Order 9397 and authorizes collection of the SSN.
PRINCIPAL PURPOSES: Documents your contract with the Air Force, specifies your contractual obligations and establishes your membership in AFROTC. Used by AFROTC to document your established commissioning date and your agreement to accept a commission, if tendered, and serve a specified period of time. The form becomes a permanent part of your master personnel record. Your Social Security Number (SSN) is used for identification and records.
ROUTINE USE: None.
DISCLOSURE IS VOLUNTARY: Failure to complete this contract may result in denial of acceptance into the AFROTC program. Disclosure of SSN is voluntary.

EXPLANATION TO THE CADET

Please read this explanation carefully. It is not a part of the contract that follows. If you want to enter into the contract that follows, you must read and understand all of its terms and conditions. If you decide to accept these terms and conditions, you will sign the contract. You will also be administered an oath of enlistment and you will sign the Enlistment/Reenlistment Document, Armed Forces of the United States (Department of Defense Form 4/1 through 4/2). If you are a minor, a parent or guardian must also sign this document. You will receive a copy of each document. Keep the copies of the documents with your important papers.

CONTRACT

STUDENT'S NAME:(Last, First, MI):	SSN:
NAME AND ADDRESS OF INSTITUTION:	DATE OF BIRTH:
	ACADEMIC MAJOR IN WHICH DEGREE IS TO BE ATTAINED:
FISCAL YEAR COMMISSION IS TO BE ADMINISTERED:	
SCHOLARSHIP PROGRAM (10 USC SECTION 2107): ☐	PROFESSIONAL OFFICER COURSE(POC)(10 USC SECTION 2104): ☐
TYPE OF SCHOLARSHIP:	LENGTH OF SCHOLARSHIP:

TYPE OF ENLISTED COMMISSIONING PROGRAM (IF APPLICABLE)(Additional requirements in AF Instructions governing such programs apply)

TYPE OF COMMISSION (1, see instruction below).	CATEGORY (2, see instruction below):	ENLISTMENT PAY GRADE/RANK

INSTRUCTIONS

1. For line officers, enter "Line." For health professions candidates, enter "Medical[(] (Nurse Corps), (Physical Therapy), (Dental), (Occupational Therapy), (Pharmacy), (Physician Assistant)", or other, as applicable]. For judge advocate selectees, enter "Law."
2. Enter "pilot," "navigator," "air battle manager," "law," approved health profession (i.e., "nurse," "pharmacy," etc) or "officer candidate," as

IMPORTANT

I UNDERSTAND THAT THE AGREEMENTS MADE IN THIS   (AF IMT1056) AND THE DD FORM 4/1 THROUGH 4/2 ARE ALL THE PROMISES MADE TO ME BY THE GOVERNMENT AND CONSTITUTE THE ENTIRE AGREEMENT. ANYTHING ELSE ANYONE HAS PROMISED ME IS NOT VALID AND WILL NOT BE HONORED, UNLESS THOSE ADDITIONAL TERMS OR REVISIONS TO THIS CONTRACT ARE MADE IN WRITING AND AGREED TO BY ME AND AN AGENT OF THE AIR FORCE WITH THE AUTHORITY TO BIND THE AIR FORCE TO THOSE ADDITIONAL TERMS.

This agreement is entered into between the Department of the Air Force and _____

hereinafter referred to as the cadet (with the consent of the parent or guardian of a minor, as defined by the laws of the state wherein the cadet is or will be enrolled), pursuant to the provisions of 10 United States Code, Sections 2104 or 2107, as implemented by DOD instructions and directives and Air Force instructions. In consideration of the mutual benefits that will accrue to the parties hereto by reason of participation in the Air Force Reserve Officer Training Corps, the parties agree as follows:

PART I - AGREEMENT OF CADET

1. I will enter into and continue military training as an AFROTC cadet under 10 U.S.C. section 2104 and/or section 2107, as applicable, unless relieved of this obligation under the provisions of instructions prescribed by the Secretary of the Air Force.

2. I will remain a full time student as defined by the academic institution listed above, pursue the degree indicated above at the academic institution listed above, pass the Air Force Officer Qualifying Test (AFOQT), and complete all AFROTC courses (or have the courses accredited by the Professor of Aerospace Studies (PAS) training (including, but not limited to, field training pursuant to 10 USC 2104 (b)(6)), and leadership laboratory requirements mandated by Air Force instructional guidance, so that I can graduate and be commissioned in the fiscal year indicated above. Any changes to these requirements must be approved in writing by the PAS at the academic institution listed above before any change is made. Making such changes prior to PAS approval may result in termination, inactivation, or suspension of financial assistance paid for my education by the Air Force (if applicable) or disenrollment from the AFROTC program and a call (or recall) to active duty for the maximum duration permitted by law or recoupment of monies expended on my education to the maximum extent permitted by law. If I am disenrolled, the decision to call (or recall) me to active duty, pursue recoupment of monies expended on my education, or release me from my obligations under this contract is within the sole discretion of the Commander, HQ AFROTC (or designee).

3. If I am contracting to pursue a degree, but have not yet been accepted into that degree program or particular school of study by the academic institution listed above (e.g., the university's school of engineering or school of pharmacy), I agree to faithfully pursue that degree by enrolling in classes required to attain that degree. If I am not accepted into that specific degree program or school within the listed academic institution's prescribed period for acceptance into such field of study or school, any financial assistance the Air Force has agreed to pay pursuant to 10 USC 2107 will be withdrawn and I may be subject to disenrollment from the AFROTC program. If, at the discretion of the Air Force, I am not disenrolled, I will not be relieved of my obligations under this contract.

4. I understand that the Secretary of the Air Force (or designee) may at any time release me without notice from obligations under this contract and separate me from the program without further benefits thereunder if, in the opinion of the Secretary of the Air Force (or designee), the best interests of the United States require such action.

5. If I am permitted to, and do, transfer to another academic institution, the provisions of this contract will remain in effect if I transfer to another institution at which an Air Force Reserve Officer Training Corps program is offered. I understand that transfer to an institution that does not offer AFROTC does not relieve me from the obligation specified in this contract.

6. If I am already a member of any military component, I will accept discharge for the convenience of the Government and will reenlist in the United States Air Force Reserve (USAFR) for the required period.

7. **Acceptance of Appointment** - I will accept an appointment as a commissioned officer in the United States Air Force upon completion of AFROTC commissioning requirements, if offered such an appointment by the Air Force. Such an offer is not guaranteed, but is contingent upon a favorable National Agency Check and/or other background inquiry; continued medical, academic, moral, and military qualification, as prescribed by law and Air Force instructional guidance; completion of all other AFROTC commissioning requirements; and the needs of the Air Force. I understand that selection as a member of the Professional Officer Course (POC) or payment of financial assistance by the Air Force pursuant to 10 USC 2107 does not bind the United States Air Force to permit my continuation as a cadet or to tender an appointment as a commissioned officer.

8. **Basic Military Service Obligation/Active Duty Service Commitment**

a. Enlistment/Basic Military Service Obligation (MSO) - As a prerequisite for membership in the AFROTC program, I will enlist in the USAFR, incurring a basic MSO of eight (8) years from the date of my enlistment, during which time I will be assigned to the Obligated Reserve Section of the Individual Ready Reserve.

b. Active Duty Service Commitment (ADSC) Upon Receipt of Appointment - Upon receiving my appointment as a commissioned officer, I will incur a four (4) year ADSC **from the date I enter onto active duty,** unless I am accepted into an Air Force program (such as Undergraduate Pilot or Navigator Training, the Health Professions Program, or any other similar program) requiring additional ADSC, in which case my ADSC will be extended as permitted by law and Air Force instructional guidance. This ADSC will run **concurrently** with my MSO, discussed above. I further understand that, if I complete the commissioning requirements through AFROTC but refuse to accept a commission, I will be subject to a call to active duty in an enlisted status for the maximum period permitted by law.

c. If the Air Force does not require fulfillment of my ADSC, and, in lieu thereof, I am ordered to active duty for training for a period less than my ADSC, I will remain a member of a Reserve or Air National Guard component until the eighth anniversary of my enlistment.

d. I understand that only the Secretary of the Air Force (or designee) may excuse me from my obligation to serve on active duty for the period specified in this contract.

e. I understand that, if I am accepted for resident graduate or professional study prior to commissioning, the Air Force may delay the start of my ADSC, based on Air Force requirements.

f. I understand that if my ADSC expires in time of war or national emergency, I may be involuntarily retained on active duty.

g. I understand that the actual date of entry on extended active duty will be determined by the Air Force based on Air Force requirements and may involve a delay of up to twelve (12) months from the date of commissioning.

9. **Nature of Military Duties/Location of Duties** - I understand that extended active duty may involve worldwide assignment or assignment to duties including, but not limited to, those involving combat or nuclear weapons. Acceptance of the terms of this agreement signifies my readiness to bear arms, to engage in or support combat operations, and to engage in or support the use of nuclear weapons. A failure to complete the program or to accept a commission because duty may involve any of the above will constitute breach of contract.

10. **Basis for Disenrollment/Result of Disenrollment** - Unless otherwise indicated in a specific subparagraph to this paragraph, disenrollment from AFROTC for failure to meet any of the below-listed standards may subject me to a call (or recall) to active duty in enlisted status for the maximum duration permitted by law or to recoupment by the Air Force of funds expended on my education to the maximum extend permitted by law. In the event of my disenrollment, the decision to call (or recall) me to active duty in my enlisted grade, pursue recoupment, or release me from my obligations under this contract is within the sole discretion of the Secretary of the Air Force (or designee). Further, disenrollment from the AFROTC may jeopardize any future opportunity I may have to obtain a commission in any United States Armed Forces.

a. Requirement to Meet Military, Academic, and Medical Retention Standards - I understand that in order to remain in the AFROTC program, I must meet or exceed all military, academic, and medical retention standards prescribed by law and Air Force instructions. Failure to meet applicable retention standards may result in my disenrollment from the AFROTC program.

b. Breach or Anticipatory Breach of Contract - I understand that if I breach, or act in a manner that demonstrates an intent to breach, as defined by Air Force instructions, this contract, I will be subject to disenrollment from the AFROTC program.

c. Demonstrated Indifference to Military Training or Environment - I understand that if I act in a manner that demonstrates an indifference to military training or apathy toward the military environment, I will be subject to disenrollment from the AFROTC program.

d. Conscientious Objector Status - If at any time I apply for conscientious objector status, I am not relieved of any obligations under this contract, regardless of the final determination on my application. I specifically understand and agree that if my application for conscientious objector status is approved, I will be required to repay all educational expenses expended on my behalf to maximum extent permitted by law.

Appendix B Activity Sheet

In the activities section of the ROTC application, candidates are asked to list any activities that they participated in and the time frame of participation. ROTC is only looking for activities/leadership/awards during the candidate's 9th, 10th, and 11th grade years. YOU ARE NOT TO INCLUDE ANTYHING FOR 12TH GRADE or anything done after the start of your senior year.

In **BOLD CAPS** are the categories of activities which candidates can add activities. You can <u>either</u> type in activities or awards or select a choice below the category and subcategory.

BOY SCOUTS
Member

CAMP FIRE
Member
          Troop Leader/Officer; Warrior Medallion

DRAMA CLUB
Actor/Actress, Stage Manager, Student Director

FOREIGN EXCHANGE STUDENT AND COUNTRY ATTENDED

GIRL SCOUTS
Member
          Bronze/Silver/Gold Award
          Troop Leader/Officer

VOLUNTEER WORK

SPORTS- SANCTIONED VARSITY SPORTS ONLY
        Baseball/Softball; Basketball; Cross Country; Fencing; Football; Golf; Gymnastics; Hockey; Judo/Karate; Lacrosse/Field Hockey; Skiing; Soccer; Swimming/Diving; Track (Indoor/Outdoor); Tennis; Volleyball; Water Polo; Wrestling

          All State
          Team Captain
          Varsity Letter Earned

SCHOOL CLUBS
National Honor Society; Student Body/Council Government

SCHOOL PUBLICATION
        Business Circulation or Advertising Manager; Editor in Chief; Feature, Sport or Photo Editor; Writer-Reporter or Other Staff Member

PRIVATE PILOTS LICENSE
Commercial; Parachuting; Private; Radio Operators License (not C.B.); Soaring

CIVIL AIR PATROL PARTICIPATION AND AWARDS
Member

SCHOOL TEAM EVENTS
Academic Bowl; Debate or Squad; Knowledge Bowl

MUSIC PARTICIPATION
Band; Chorus; Drill (JROTC not included); Orchestra

WORK
Jobs During the School Year; Summer Jobs
1-9 Hours per week; 10-19 Hours per week; 20-29 Hours per week; 30-39 Hours per week; 40+ Hours per week

NON SCHOOL CLUBS
4H/FFA; Big Brother/Sister; Boys/Girls State; Boys/Girls Nation; Camp Counselor; Church Group; Decca; Junior Achievement; Model UN/Mock Trial/Toastmasters; National Beta Club

Appendix C Interview Questions and Scoring

1. Character/Core Values: Military officers do the right thing for the right reasons, all the time. It means doing the right thing whether someone is watching or not. They are loyal first to the Constitution and nation, then to the institutional Air Force, then to their units, then to their wingmen, and finally to themselves. They do not tolerate deviations from what is right from subordinates, peers, superiors or friends.

*These questions should help you evaluate the interviewee's **character/core values.***

Question. What does integrity mean to you?

Example answer and scoring: —Somebody with integrity knows the difference between right and wrong, but there are times when it's really complicated. On big, obvious things you absolutely need to do the right thing, but when it's a little thing, or your friends are involved, and nobody could possibly know what you did, then it's probably ok to cut some corners.

Scoring: This kind of answer is indicative of an applicant who is in need of character development and a 2 would be appropriate. [see benchmarks below]

Another example answer and scoring: —To me, integrity means doing the right thing whether anyone is watching or not. It means doing the right thing for the right reasons, all the time. It means telling the truth about something you did even if it results in your getting into trouble. It means being willing to come forward and report what a friend did, even if doing so results in losing that friend, or being ostracized from a group of friends. *Scoring:* This kind of answer shows an advanced understanding of integrity and what it takes to live according to the AF core values and if combined with indications that the applicant has lived IAW this definition of integrity (see question 1-2) is deserving of a 4 or a 5.

Question 1-2. Tell me about a time when a friend did something wrong? How did you react? What did you do as a consequence? [If the applicant can't cite an example then pose ask them to respond to the question hypothetically.]

Example answer and scoring: Once my friend offered me the answers to our math test, but even though I knew that I was going to struggle on the test and even though I knew that I wouldn't have been caught, I turned my friend down and didn't take the answers to the test.

Scoring: This kind of answer suggests that the person deserves a score of at least a 3, and maybe even a 4 or a 5 since the stakes were high and the chance of getting caught was low, especially if the applicant gave a good definition for integrity.

Another example answer and scoring: I was walking home once and these local guys were all picking on this really awkward kid at the bus stop (I didn't know him), and even though I was worried that it might cause a confrontation, I stepped in an stood up for him and waited with him until the guys left.

Scoring: This kind of answer shows excellent character since the applicant made the right choice even though they knew it would be unpopular with the local guys, could have come at personal harm to them, and the only gain was the knowledge that they did the right thing. If the applicant can give several completely different high quality examples then they would be deserving of 4 or a 5, especially in combination with a good definition of integrity.

2. Self Confidence: Military officers are self-confident. They are confident in their ability to accomplish assigned missions and their ability to control themselves. They project a calm, unflappable, martial image regardless how challenging the environment so as to inspire confidence among their subordinates. Military officers know how to be, and are, in charge when appropriate.

*Ask the following questions of the applicant to give them a chance to talk about a comfortable subject, themselves. Observe the verbal and non-verbal cues they present during their responses, in combination with the manner in which they introduced themselves to you and how they conducted themselves throughout the interview to assess their **self-confidence**. Take notes and then score the applicant using the rating standard below.*

Question 2-1. What are your major interests? Hobbies?

Notes of applicant's responses:

Bearing/Posture:

Eye contact:

Tone of voice and delivery:

Quality of answers: Full and intended to engage/inform the interviewer? Or, brief and hoping to get through the interview?

First impression at introduction: Good handshake/greeting? Did you get the sense that they wanted to be there and to impress?

Question 2-2. What are the priorities in your life? What do you truly care about?

Notes of applicant's responses:

Bearing/Posture:

Eye contact:

Tone of voice and delivery:

Quality of answers: Full and intended to engage/inform the interviewer? Or, brief and hoping to get through the interview?

First impression at introduction: Good handshake/greeting? Did you get the sense that they wanted to be there and to impress?

3. **Human Relations:** Military officers are comfortable working in teams and they value the inherent strengths that come from teams made up of people with different backgrounds and perspectives. They are respectful of others. They understand that high performing teams are characterized by common goals, shared responsibility for success and appropriate leadership-followership relationships.

*These questions should help you evaluate the interviewee's **human relations skills**.*

Question 3-1. When someone gives you a big, complex project to accomplish do you prefer to do it by yourself, or do you prefer to do it with a group of people? Ask why their preference is to work independently or with a group. Ask them to provide examples of projects they have done as a group member and what those experiences taught them about working in groups.

Example answer and scoring: —I would always prefer to work by myself than in a group. Groups are inefficient. Whenever I have been in a group I have done all of the work and had to share the credit. Working in a group would be ok, except some kinds of people are just lazy. Yes, I can give you an example of when I worked in a group. Just last month I had to work on a science project for my Governor's School Physics class. It taught me not to work in groups. There were three of us trying to develop and all-terrain baby stroller and we failed because one of the other kids was stubborn and wouldn't do it my way, so we failed.

Scoring: This answer shows an inability to recognize the benefit of working in teams and of teamwork. Further, it hints at poor interpersonal skills and poor self-awareness which are essential to working effectively with others. This answer would be deserving of a 1, or perhaps a 2 if the applicant gave a homerun response to question 3-2.

Another example answer and scoring: —Unless the project needed to be done right away I would always prefer to work as part of a group. Why? Well, I have done a number of involved projects—I just finished my Girl Scout Gold Award project where my Troop and I put up 115 blue bird boxes in 6 county parks—and I have found that collectively we are better than we are individually. By this I mean that when a number of people work on

37

a project they bring diverse experiences to the group and we're more often going to build on each other's suggestions to get a great answer instead of just an ok answer to a problem.

Scoring: This answer demonstrates a sound mastery of group dynamics and a high-level of human relations skills. The applicant has learned when groups, teams, are especially effective and how to use/function within them. This response is indicative of a 4 or a 5; a clear 5 with a solid response to question 3-2.

Question 3-2. Tell me about a situation you were involved in that consisted of a very different or diverse environment (either culturally, ethnically, or religiously), and what you learned from this experience. Ask if the group would have worked better if it was made-up of people just like themselves.

Example answer and scoring: —I attended American Legion Boy's State last summer. It was a good program and I learned a lot about how state government works. The boys came from all over our state and they were of difference races and religions and even different economic classes. I pretty much got along with everyone, except for the guys from the city. They were just so different from me and from my friends that I couldn't relate to them; couldn't agree with them on anything. The guys from farm country were different too, but we got along ok, and we passed some legislation that benefitted my Boy's State city; that was good.

Scoring: This answer shows an applicant with average, to below average human relations skills. There was evidence of both tolerance and intolerance of others. The response points to a modest-level of effectiveness working in a team and focusing on achieving group goals. This answer would be deserving of a 2 or a 3. The applicant's responses point to a pretty self-centered individual who can get along if they want to and if it benefits them. A 3 would only be warranted if this answer was paired with a strong answer to question 3-1.

Another example answer and scoring: —I spent last summer in Nicaragua; three weeks in an intensive Spanish language program and two months living with a Nicaraguan family in the country. While I was in the country I was working with an NGO that was fielding small-scale alternative energy projects that people could us, for example I helped develop an apparatus that fermented chicken manure into methane gas for cooking. Not headline grabbing stuff, but it worked very well for these folks. I learned an incredible amount. I learned that people are people wherever you go. We may look different, we may talk different, we may have some different ideas, but we're all basically the same and should treat each other with dignity and respect.

Scoring: This answer demonstrates a sound mastery of group dynamics and a high-level of human relations skills. The applicant has learned when groups, teams, are especially effective and how to use/function within them. This response is indicative of a 4 or a 5; a clear 5 with a solid response to question 3-2.

4. Planning and Organizing: Military officers get things done. They are able determine how best to divide large tasks into smaller parts and then develop plans to accomplish them. They are able to set priorities and manage their time accordingly, then organize themselves and others to accomplish the priority tasks. Then, they relentlessly apply themselves until they get the job done.

*These questions should help you evaluate the interviewee's **planning and organization**.*

Question 4-1. Here's your résumé. Please review it, then describe for me a time when you had a big, complex project to accomplish. Tell me how you planned and organized your efforts to finish the project, how you stayed on task, what the outcome was, and what you learned from it.

Example answer and scoring: —I am the Vice-President of my high school's chapter of the National Honor Society and was responsible for organizing our induction ceremony for new members. It's really the biggest thing we do in Honor Society each year. I got the list of the kids that were to become members, then we set up a date and contacted the Principal and our Advisor so they could attend. I had plans to make it real special, but I got busy with other things—other clubs and school—and kind of got rushed at the end. It turned out ok because my mom and the Advisor tied-up a few loose ends at the last minute.

Scoring: There is little evidence of planning and organization ability in this response. The applicant provided an example, but it was one that showed poor task prioritization and organization skills and the need to be helped out end-game by parent and teacher. This answer deserves a 2 in isolation. If there are other, better examples, and/or a very good response to question 4-3, then it could warrant a 3.

Another example answer and scoring: —That's an easy one. I started off poorly in my calculus class last semester. I knew that I could do better. So I gave up playing football; I just had too much on my plate. Then I developed a disciplined study schedule and attended weekly tutoring three times a week in the evenings. I had to work real hard to dig out of the hole—studying nights and weekends—but I did and it worked. I managed to pull my grade up from a D to an A.

Scoring: This is a very good answer. The respondent took on a significant task, made difficult prioritization decisions, then developed and followed a good plan using excellent time management to achieve their goal. They then worked diligently to execute that plan. This answer is deserving of a 3, or 4, or is possibly the foundation of a 5 if the applicant has more, similar examples, and/or they provide a good response to question 4-3.

Question 4-3. Can you give me an example of when you had too much to do? How did you resolve the conflicts in your schedule? How did you establish priorities for your efforts?

Example answer and scoring: —Sure, this seems like the story of my life. I stay very busy between all of the AP courses I take, year round sports that I play, many school clubs that I belong to and being the Senior Class Treasurer. It's funny, but I always find a way. There are times when I just think I can't do it all, but I always seem to pull it out. It helps to use a day planner to help manage.

Scoring: This response seems to indicate that the respondent really was not tested—that they didn't have too much to do—or that they failed to recognize and respond to being over-committed. The reference to use of a day planner is very good though. This answer is deserving of 2 in isolation, perhaps a 3 if there a solid example in response to questions 4-1.

Another example answer and scoring: —Yes I can. I really got in over my head spring of my Junior year. I was taking mostly IB classes, playing soccer, and working two evenings a week. My grades began to suffer and I was not sleeping enough. I felt out of control. So I stepped back and asked myself what was important to me. The answer was my family and school since they would determine my future. So I gave up soccer and talked to my boss about working only on Saturdays. Then I cut out wasted time watching TV and closed down my Facebook account to make the most of the time I scheduled to study. It was a great experience. It helped me figure out what is really important to me, gave me some tools to use when I need to re-orient my priorities, and gave me some good study habits for when I go away to college.

Scoring: This is a very good answer. The respondent recognized the barriers to their success, and that only they could overcome them, then they made difficult prioritization decisions, and followed through on them. This answer is deserving of a 4, or is possibly the foundation of a 5 if the applicant provided good answers to questions 4-1 and/or 4-2.

5. Communication Skills: Military officers are clear verbal communicators. They recognize that clear communication requires effective listening, careful thought, and articulate and appropriate responses. They have an exceptional verbal delivery.

*Ask the following questions of the applicant to give them a chance to talk about a comfortable subject, themselves. Observe the verbal responses they present during their responses, in combination with the manner in which they introduced themselves to you and how they responded throughout the interview to assess their **communication skills**. Take notes and then score the applicant using the rating standard below.*

Question 5-1. Please describe for me a frustrating experience you faced and how you handled it.

Notes on applicant's response:

Did they listen to your question and answer appropriately?

Articulate responses (Vocabulary; Use of slang)

Verbal delivery

Question 5-2. If you could start your education over again, what would you change or do differently?

Did they listen to your question and answer appropriately?

Articulate responses (Vocabulary; Use of slang)

Verbal delivery

Leadership: Military officers are effective leaders. They are skilled at influencing and directing others in order to accomplish a task. They have a knack for employing group problem-solving, developing commitment from teammates, delegating and following-up on tasks, and motivating the people they work with to accomplish a group goal.

*These questions should help you evaluate the interviewee's **leadership**.* [You should strive to have multiple examples of leadership accomplishments for the most highly qualified applicants.]

Question 6-1. Let's review your résumé again. Last time we were looking at it for examples of significant accomplishments, this time I'd like to focus on things you did that showed leadership, where you worked through others to accomplish something. With that in mind, please tell me about an activity in which you served as a formal or informal leader.

Example answer and scoring: —I was the captain of my high school football team this last year. I was the best player so most of the guys looked up to me. Whenever we got behind because we were not following the game plan or weren't hustling I turned to John, our tight end—John's a real sharp guy and an ok player—he always knew exactly what to say, to whom, to get things back on track.

Scoring: There is little evidence of real leadership ability in this response. The applicant provided an example, but on reflection, one that showed he lacked the ability to influence or motivate his teammates to win. This answer deserves a 1 or a 2 in isolation. If there are other, better examples, then it could warrant a 2 or a 3.

Another example answer and scoring: —I was the Patrol Leader for a 125 mile Boy Scout backpacking trip. I had to work with the guys to organize the Patrol, plan the trip to include the route we would follow, where we would camp, where we could get water, all of that. Then, once on the trail, I had to assign daily tasks, trying to balance the workload and encourage the guys to keep going to stay on schedule; this required buy-in from the other guys. Sometimes it was a challenge to keep them all hiking, but I did so by telling them they needed to do their part if we were to be successful. The trip was a great success and we all learned a lot.

Scoring: This is a very good answer. The respondent took the initiative on a significant task, worked through his fellow scouts to develop a plan they all bought in to. Then he had to coach, cajole, and motivate his Patrol on the trail. This answer is deserving of a 4, or is possibly the foundation of a 5 if the applicant has more, similar examples.

Question 6-2. Thanks. That was great. Can you give me another example, perhaps one based on a different interest area highlighted on your résumé? I see that you have done some great things with…

Example answer and scoring: For the last three years, I have worked as a life guard at the local swimming pool, mostly during the summer. Last summer I was made the head life guard. As the head life guard I had to build the life guard schedule and supervise the rest of the guards at the pool, making sure they were trained, carefully watched the pool and enforced the rules so that everything stayed safe.

Scoring: This response includes several of the elements important to leadership—responsibility and implicit ability to direct others—but it leaves out others—initiative, motivation, inspiration, etc. As such, this is solid three by itself.

Another example answer and scoring: I put on the inaugural leukemia fund raising tennis tournament at my high school. Through my, and my teammate's, efforts we raised $67,000 to benefit cancer research in honor of a classmate that died of leukemia last year. To do this I spoke with my coach and principal, then the school board to get permission; then I enlisted my teammates help to organize the tournament at a local country club. I delegated contacting the local TV and radio stations and newspaper to advertise the tournament to three of my teammates. Several adults asked if they would help and I assigned them the job of soliciting prizes. On the day of the tournament my teammates oversaw the competition and helped the umpires keep the matches fair. It was such a success that the school decided to hold this event each year. It taught me a lot about how to influence people, some older to you, to accomplish an important event.

Scoring: Clearly this is a very good response. The applicant showed initiative, a willingness to fearlessly take-on responsibility, the ability to delegate and follow-up on important tasks, and a knack for motivating others. This response alone is worthy of a 4 rating, with other solid examples, this could easily be a 5.

7. Motivation toward the Air Force: The path to an Air Force officer's commission through AFROTC is challenging. A cadet has to complete a rigorous undergraduate program while they are learning the distinctly military elements of their chosen career. Success takes drive and motivation.

*This question should help you evaluate the interviewee's **motivation toward the Air Force**.*

Why do you want to be an Air Force officer?

Example answer and scoring: —My family has a longstanding tradition of the men graduating from A&M; it's a good school with an outstanding Corps of Cadets. We're not residents and —out-of-state tuition is too much for me to pay, but if you're on an ROTC scholarship you can attend A&M at the —in-state tuition rate. And I think being an Air Force officer will give me some good skills for when my commitment is up. *Scoring:* There are many reasons to want to be an Air Force officer and a willingness to serve the minimal commitment in order to have the cost of college paid for is not a bad one, but is indicative of a 3 rating.

Another example answer and scoring: —When I was seven I saw the Thunderbirds fly. It was the most amazing demonstration of skill, bravery, and combat power I have ever seen. From that moment I have known I wanted to be an Air Force officer. I joined Civil Air Patrol as soon as I could and did a little light aircraft flying and I spent all four of my high school years in JROTC. I am the Cadet Wing Commander. These two activities introduced me to the Air Force and Air Force officers and gave me a chance to get a sense of the responsibilities associated with being an officer. I have taken lots of math and science in school because I know the Air Force needs officers with STEM degrees. While I'll do whatever the Air Force wants me to do, I really want to be an F-22 pilot *Scoring:* Wants to be an American Fighter Pilot; easily a 5.

Appendix D Air Force ROTC PFA Certification Form

AIR FORCE ROTC SCHOLARSHIP PHYSICAL FITNESS ASSESSMENT (PFA) CERTIFICATION FORM

Description
Air Force ROTC require High School Scholarship applicants to complete a Physical Fitness Assessment (PFA) and record the results using this certification form. The PFA consists of three events: one-minute push-ups, one-minute sit-ups, and a 1.5 mile run. There is a rest period of up to five (5) minutes in between events. Upon completion, scan and upload form to your online application at https://wings.holmcenter.com by 11:59pm Central Time on 31 JANUARY 2019

AFROTC Applicant Information

Name:			Date of Birth:	Gender:	Age:	Ht (in):	Wt (lbs):

High School:

☐	I certify that I, the applicant named above, do not have any current or pre-existing medical conditions and that I am not taking any medications which would preclude me from participating in, and completing the PFA. I am in good health and I do not suffer from any physical illness or injury.
☐	I am requesting an exemption from taking the PFA due to a documented physical injury (i.e., a broken leg, arm, mono, etc.), which preclude me from completing the PFA. I have attached a letter from my doctor with my full name, date of birth, address, and a description of my injury/illness.

Applicant Signature/Date:	Parent/Legal Guardian Signature/Date: (Required for applicants under 18 years of age)

Test Administrator Information (ONLY high school officials may administer the Physical Fitness Assessment (PFA) and certify results.

Name:		Title:		Test Date:
Telephone/Email: (___) ___ - ____		Signature:		

Air Force ROTC Physical Fitness Assessment Instructions

Push-Up Event (1 Minute)	Sit-Up Event (1 Minute)	Run Event (1.5 Mile)
Instructions: The start position begins with the hands shoulder width apart, elbows fully extended, body straight and feet together or up to 12 inches apart. To complete a repetition, the applicant lowers his/her body, maintaining a straight back, until the upper arm is parallel with ground, then returns to the start position. Once the one-minute push-up period has started, candidate may not lift their arms or legs off the ground. They may rest in the "start" position. They may also bend at the waist and the knees to relax the back, always maintaining 4-point contact with the ground. Before resuming push-ups, they must return to the "start" position.	Instructions: The start position is lying on the floor with face up, knees bent at a 90-degree angle, and feet/heels in contact with the floor at all times. The heels and buttocks must remain on the floor during the entire assessment. The applicant's arms will be crossed over the chest with the hands at the shoulders or resting on the upper chest. A complete crunch is accomplished when the upper torso of the applicant is raised off the floor, the elbows touch the knees or thighs, and the upper torso is lowered back to the floor until the shoulder blades touch the floor. The hands must stay in contact with the shoulders/upper chest at all times. Once the one-minute crunch period has started, the applicant may only rest in the up position. If the applicant rests in the down position, the test will be terminated. The applicant may secure their feet under a stationary object or have an observer hold their feet (no higher than the ankles).	Instructions: The 1.5-mile run must be performed on a measured track or course. The applicant may walk during the event, as long as they stay on the track/ course. The applicant may not receive physical assistance from anyone while performing the event, however, verbal encouragement is acceptable. DO NOT USE A TREADMILL
Number of Repetitions:	Number of Repetitions:	Time:____Min____Sec

Appendix E Medical Qualification Flow Chart

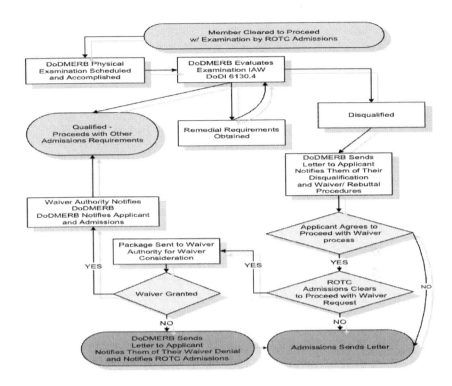

1899

A Message to Garcia

By Elbert Hubbard

In all this Cuban business there is one man stands out on the horizon of my memory like Mars at perihelion. When war broke out between Spain & the United States, it was very necessary to communicate quickly with the leader of the Insurgents. Garcia was somewhere in the mountain vastness of Cuba- no one knew where. No mail nor telegraph message could reach him. The President must secure his cooperation, and quickly.

What to do!

Someone said to the President, "There's a fellow by the name of Rowan will find Garcia for you, if anybody can."

Rowan was sent for and given a letter to be delivered to Garcia. How "the fellow by the name of Rowan" took the letter, sealed it up in an oil-skin pouch, strapped it over his heart, in four days landed by night off the coast of Cuba from an open boat, disappeared into the jungle, & in three weeks came out on the other side of the Island, having traversed a hostile country on foot, and delivered his letter to Garcia, are things I have no special desire now to tell in detail.

The point I wish to make is this: McKinley gave Rowan a letter to be delivered to Garcia; Rowan took the letter and did not ask, "Where is he at?" By the Eternal! there is a man whose form should be cast in deathless bronze and the statue placed in every college of the land. It is not book-learning young men need, nor instruction about this and that, but a stiffening of the vertebrae which will cause them to be loyal to a trust, to act promptly, concentrate their energies: do the thing- "Carry a message to Garcia!"

General Garcia is dead now, but there are other Garcias.

No man, who has endeavored to carry out an enterprise where many hands were needed, but has been well-nigh appalled at times by the imbecility of the average man- the inability or unwillingness to concentrate on a thing and do it. Slip-shod assistance, foolish inattention, dowdy indifference, & half-hearted work seem the rule; and no man succeeds, unless by hook or crook, or threat, he forces or bribes other men to assist him; or mayhap, God in His goodness performs a miracle, & sends him an Angel of Light for an assistant. You, reader, put this matter to a test: You are sitting now in your office- six clerks are within call.

Summon any one and make this request: "Please look in the encyclopedia and make a brief memorandum for me concerning the life of Correggio".

Will the clerk quietly say, "Yes, sir," and go do the task?

On your life, he will not. He will look at you out of a fishy eye and ask one or more of the following questions:

Who was he?

Which encyclopedia?

Where is the encyclopedia?

Was I hired for that?

Don't you mean Bismarck?

What's the matter with Charlie doing it?

Is he dead?

Is there any hurry?

Shan't I bring you the book and let you look it up yourself?

What do you want to know for?

And I will lay you ten to one that after you have answered the questions, and explained how to find the information, and why you want it, the clerk will go off and get one of the other clerks to help him try to find Garcia- and then come back and tell you there is no such man. Of course I may lose my bet, but according to the Law of Average, I will not.

Now if you are wise you will not bother to explain to your "assistant" that Correggio is indexed under the C's, not in the K's, but you will smile sweetly and say, "Never mind," and go look it up yourself.

And this incapacity for independent action, this moral stupidity, this infirmity of the will, this unwillingness to cheerfully catch hold and lift, are the things that put pure Socialism so far into the future. If men will not act for themselves, what will they do when the benefit of their effort is for all? A first-mate with knotted club seems necessary; and the dread of getting "the bounce" Saturday night, holds many a worker to his place.

Advertise for a stenographer, and nine out of ten who apply, can neither spell nor punctuate- and do not think it necessary to.

Can such a one write a letter to Garcia?

"You see that bookkeeper," said the foreman to me in a large factory.

"Yes, what about him?"

"Well he's a fine accountant, but if I'd send him up town on an errand, he might accomplish the errand all right, and on the other hand, might stop at four saloons on the way, and when he got to Main Street, would forget what he had been sent for."

Can such a man be entrusted to carry a message to Garcia?

We have recently been hearing much maudlin sympathy expressed for the "downtrodden denizen of the sweat-shop" and the "homeless wanderer searching for honest employment," & with it all often go many hard words for the men in power.

Nothing is said about the employer who grows old before his time in a vain attempt to get frowsy ne'er-do-wells to do intelligent work; and his long patient striving with "help" that does nothing but loaf when his back is turned. In every store and factory there is a constant weeding-out process going on. The employer is constantly sending away "help" that have shown their incapacity to further the interests of the business, and others are being taken on. No matter how good times are, this sorting continues, only if times are hard and work is scarce, the sorting is done finer- but out and forever out, the incompetent and unworthy go.

It is the survival of the fittest. Self-interest prompts every employer to keep the best-those who can carry a message to Garcia.

I know one man of really brilliant parts who has not the ability to manage a business of his own, and yet who is absolutely worthless to anyone else, because he carries with him constantly the insane suspicion that his employer is oppressing, or intending to oppress him. He cannot give orders; and he will not receive them. Should a message be given him to take to Garcia, his answer would probably be, "Take it yourself."

Tonight this man walks the streets looking for work, the wind whistling through his threadbare coat. No one who knows him dare employ him, for he is a regular fire-brand of discontent. He is impervious to reason, and the only thing that can impress him is the toe of a thick-soled No. 9 boot.

Of course I know that one so morally deformed is no less to be pitied than a physical cripple; but in our pitying, let us drop a tear, too, for the men who are striving to carry on a great enterprise, whose working hours are not limited by the whistle, and whose hair is fast turning white through the struggle to hold in line dowdy indifference, slip-shod imbecility, and the heartless ingratitude, which, but for their enterprise, would be both hungry & homeless.

Have I put the matter too strongly? Possibly I have; but when all the world has gone a-slumming I wish to speak a word of sympathy for the man who succeeds- the man who, against great odds has directed the efforts of others, and having succeeded, finds there's nothing in it: nothing but bare board and clothes.

I have carried a dinner pail & worked for day's wages, and I have also been an employer of labor, and I know there is something to be said on both sides. There is no excellence, per se, in poverty; rags are no recommendation; & all employers are not rapacious and high-handed, any more than all poor men are virtuous.

My heart goes out to the man who does his work when the "boss" is away, as well as when he is at home. And the man who, when given a letter for Garcia, quietly take the missive, without asking any idiotic questions, and with no lurking intention of chucking it into the nearest sewer, or of doing aught else but deliver it, never gets "laid off," nor has to go on a strike for higher wages. Civilization is one long anxious search for just such individuals. Anything such a man asks shall be granted; his kind is so rare that no employer can afford to let him go. He is wanted in every city, town and village- in every office, shop, store and factory. The world cries out for such: he is needed, & needed badly- the man who can carry a message to Garcia.

THE END-

Appendix G Frequently Asked Questions about ROTC Consulting Services

Question: When is the timeframe we should begin to inquire about your consulting services?

Answer: Generally, the Air Force ROTC scholarship application opens online in July for rising seniors in high school. You should contact me between April and November to start application process so that you can be evaluated by the Services for the ROTC scholarship in the Fall or latest after the first of the year.

Question: What is the difference between what is presented in your "Insider's Guide" book I am reading here and what you provide with your consulting services?

Answer: My consulting services are helpful in a number of ways. Clients state that the interview preparation via video conferencing and scholarship essay review are the two most important services I provide outside of the book.

Question: Aside from interview preparation and essay review, what other areas do you help with in the process?

Answer: I help with all areas of the application. Maximizing the point totals, advising whether to retake standardized tests, help with any psychological testing, general medical questions, best fit schools where scholarship benefits can be maximized, and connecting the applicant with currently serving officers and ROTC cadets to learn more about life as a cadet/midshipman and future officer.

Question: Are there any other services than individual consulting?

Answer: We have an instructional video course with a monthly zoom session with LTC Kirkland to answer questions and provide insight on the course. This video course is free if a client pays for individual consulting.

Question: How is your experience as a former Professor of Military Science helpful in connecting with ROTC programs?

Answer: As a military officer and a person knowledgeable about ROTC, I am able to call individual university ROTC programs and "talk the lingo" about ROTC and find out information about specific programs that a candidate would not otherwise be able to determine. I can also talk directly to the ROTC Service component headquarters to help ease the application process.

Question: Do you also work with candidates who are interested in the Service Academies?

Answer: Yes! We are experts on the Service Academy admissions process. You can purchase our books on the Air Force Academy, the Naval Academy and West Point at this link: https://www.gainserviceacademyadmission.com/book/

Question: Where can I view some testimonials regarding your consulting services?

Answer: Visit the ROTC Consulting You Tube page at: https://www.youtube.com/channel/UCzTiJwdQoHFDpDftQLCTR5A?view_as=subscriber

Question: Do you have a website?

Answer: Visit the ROTC Consulting at: https://rotcconsulting.com.There you will find our podcast as well as our blog and other pertinent information.

Made in the USA
Middletown, DE
04 April 2022

63592737R00029